Tom Wolfe Carves
SPIRIT CANES

Tom Wolfe

Schiffer Publishing Ltd®

4880 Lower Valley Road Atglen, Pennsylvania 19310

Other Schiffer Books by Tom Wolfe

Carving Canes & Walking Sticks with Tom Wolfe. Size: 8 1/2" x 11" ■ 200 color photos, patterns, gallery ■ 48 pp.ISBN: 0-88740-587-8 ■ soft cover ■ $12.95

Carving Fancy Walking Sticks.
Size: 8 1/2" x 11" ■ 200 color photos ■ 64 pp.
ISBN: 0-7643-1565-X ■ soft cover ■ $14.95

Carving a Friendship Cane.
Size: 8 1/2" x 11" ■ 250 color photos■ 64 pp.
ISBN: 0-88740-891-5 ■ soft cover ■ $12.95

Creative Canes & Walking Sticks: Carving with Tom Wolfe. Size: 8 1/2" x 11" ■ 250 color photos
11 patterns ■ 64 pp.
ISBN: 0-88740-885-0 ■ soft cover ■ $12.95

86 Cane Patterns for the Woodcarver.
Size: 8 1/2" x 11" ■ 86 patterns ■ 64 pp.
ISBN: 0-7643-0372-4 ■ soft cover ■ $14.95

Tom Wolfe Carves Fancy Canes.
Size: 8 1/2" x 11" ■ 162 color photos ■ 48 pp.
ISBN: 0-7643-1343-6 ■ soft cover ■ $14.95

Designed by Stephanie Daugherty
Type set in Zurich BT
ISBN: 978-0-7643-3051-3
Printed in China

Schiffer Books are available at special discounts for bulk purchases for sales promotions or premiums. Special editions, including personalized covers, corporate imprints, and excerpts can be created in large quantities for special needs. For more information contact the publisher:

Published by Schiffer Publishing Ltd.
4880 Lower Valley Road
Atglen, PA 19310
Phone: (610) 593-1777
Fax: (610) 593-2002
E-mail: Info@schifferbooks.com

For the largest selection of fine reference books on this and related subjects, please visit our web site at
www.schifferbooks.com
We are always looking for people to write books on new and related subjects. If you have an idea for a book please contact us at the above address.

This book may be purchased from the publisher.
Include $5.00 for shipping.
Please try your bookstore first.
You may write for a free catalog.

In Europe, Schiffer books are distributed by
Bushwood Books
6 Marksbury Ave.
Kew Gardens
Surrey TW9 4JF England
Phone: 44 (0) 20 8392-8585t
Fax: 44 (0) 20 8392-9876
E-mail: info@bushwoodbooks.co.uk
Website: www.bushwoodbooks.co.uk
Free postage in the U.K., Europe; air mail at cost.

Introduction

I don't know why canes are so popular, but of all the things I've carved over the years they are among those that draw the highest interest. It's hard to keep them in my shop.

Maybe it's the Spirits that live in the wood. They always seem to be there, just waiting to come out. And they are fun to uncover. The carvings usually are done near the root ball of the sapling, so there are bumps and voids that give great interest to the carving. And sometimes, like the rock held in place in the root carved in this book, there are surprises that add even more interest to the work.

Maybe one of the reasons the canes are so popular is that every cane is unique. No two are alike! And each sapling calls forth a different Spirit. For the carver this is a bit of a challenge. You need to learn the basic techniques well enough that you can apply them to the particular sapling you are working with.

There is also the possibility of hidden surprises within the wood. In the sapling use for the project in this book, a vein of dark wood ran just under the surface, showing itself when I started to gouge out space for the eyes. It looked like the wood spirit had been in a pretty good fight...and was the loser!

I suppose I could have started over (though my photographer would not have been happy), but chose instead to go ahead, and then show how the problem could be solved in the finishing. I hope it helps you.

Because each sapling is unique, patterns are not of much use in this kind of carving. Of far more importance is a basic approach to wood, seeing the figure in it, doing the basic drawing, and carving it.

I hope this book will lead to hours of enjoyment. Happy carving!

For a "found" cane, the root makes for a stylish handle with a natural look. I usually find these growing on a slope because the tap root seems to turn at a better in that situation, making a more handle-like angle.
This particular root has grown around a stone. If I can keep it in the wood and work around it, I'll end up with a nice accent to the cane handle.

Trim off the hair roots. For the smaller cuts a knife works pretty well for this task.

4

Progress. The major root tap at the left will make the cane handle.

The other major root I take off with a bandsaw.

Shorten the handle to a manageable length.

5

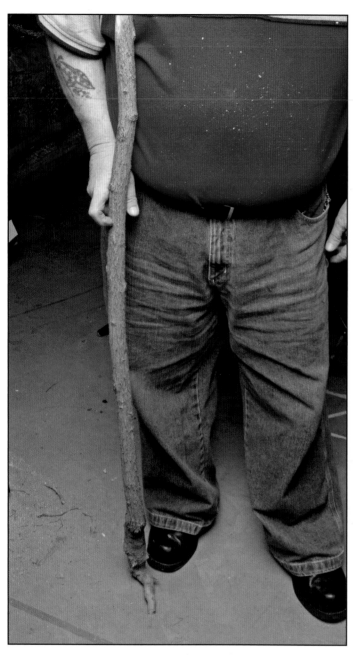

The length of the cane is measured by holding it upside down and determining a comfortable handle position. I like it just below the belt line. Mark the spot length…

and chop it off at the bandsaw.

The cross section reveals the white wood of the sassafras, with a orange bark subsurface. This will come into play when we carve, providing some nice color. We can also see some dark growth rings. These are usually not a problem, but we shall see.

The first step is to trim the bark off the handle…

and the stick.

With sassafras, like this, you can gently scrape off the upper surface of the bark to leave a red undersurface. With oil this will turn a nice shade of red.

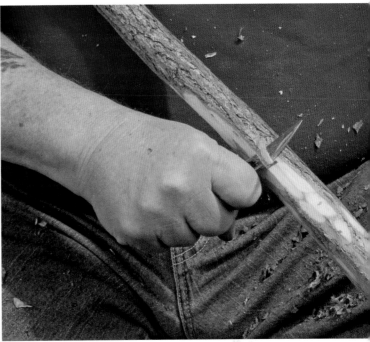

At the lower end I'll do a complete skinning again. I want to taper this lower portion more that it is.

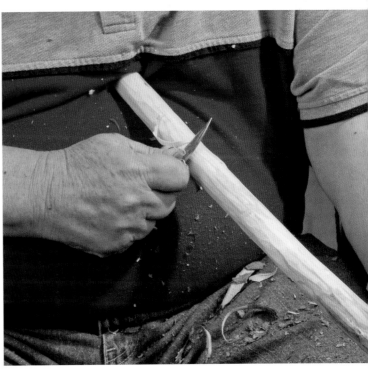

With the lower portion stripped I can start tapering.

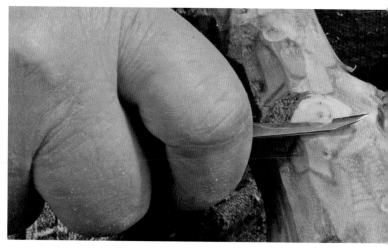

I like to smooth off some of these bumps but leave others. It's all a matter of what pleases your eye.

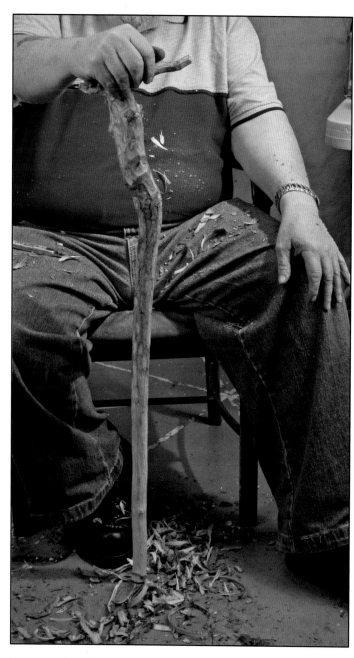

Progress. Now I need to decide where to put the face.

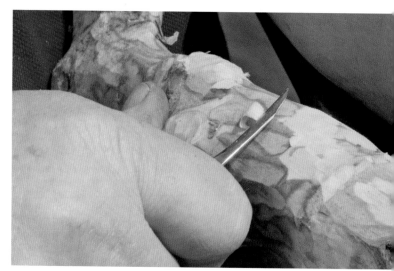

Clean up the area below the handle.

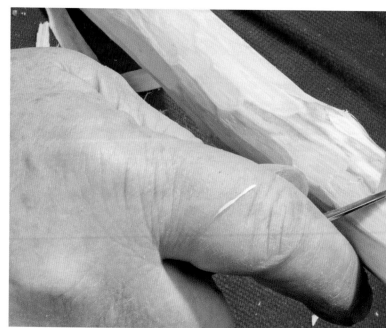

That done, I want to work on the lower end to taper it even more.

Ready for carving.

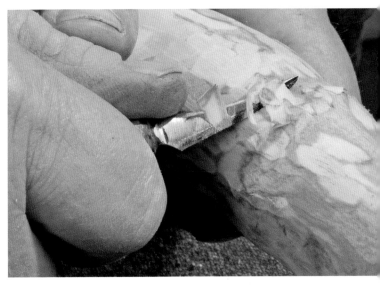

Clean the area for the face.

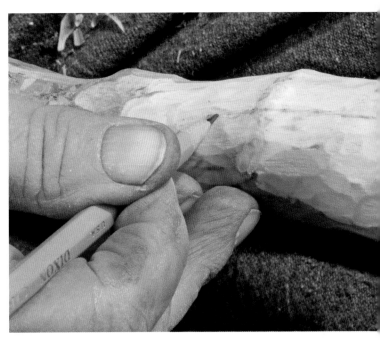

Make a center mark.

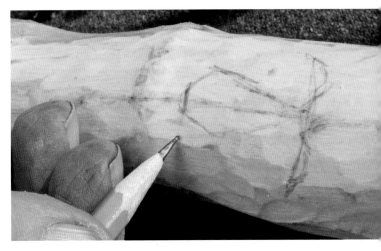

Mark the nose and brow line

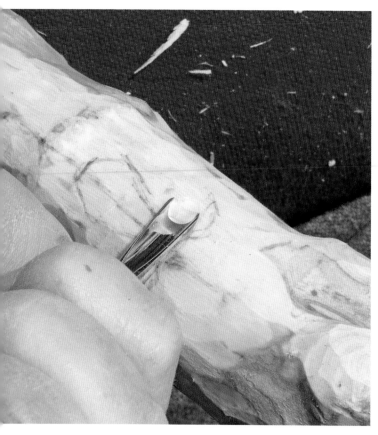 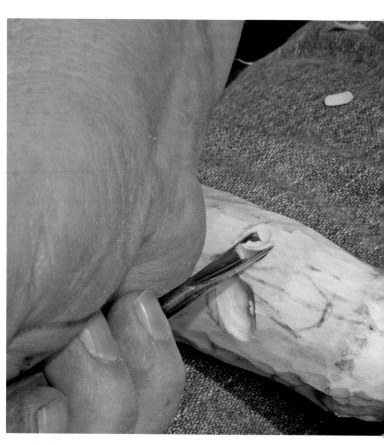

Use a gouge to make the eye socket. Work out from the center … in both directions. I am going deep enough to bring out the nose.

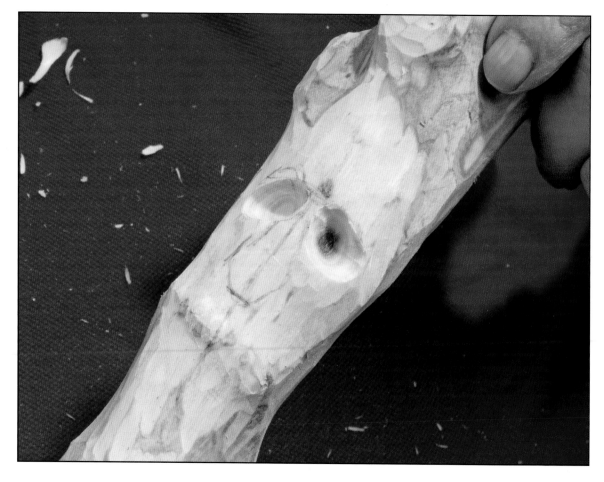

The result.

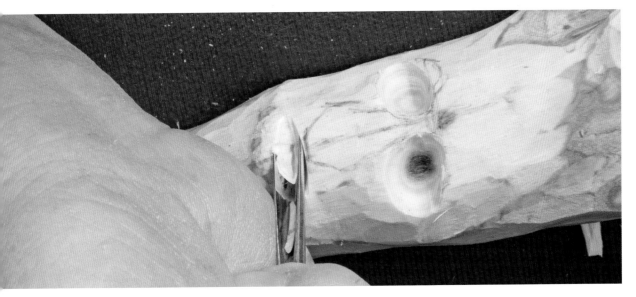

Run a v-tool under the nose to bring it out.

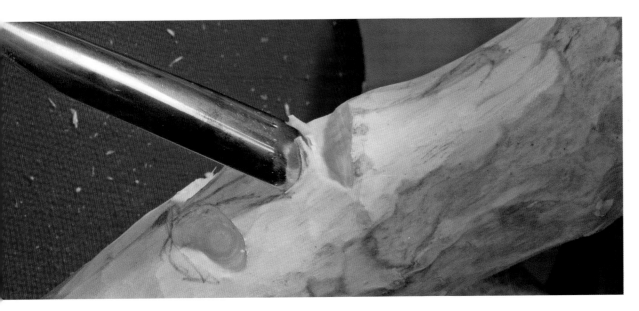

Make a stop cut with a chisel under the nose

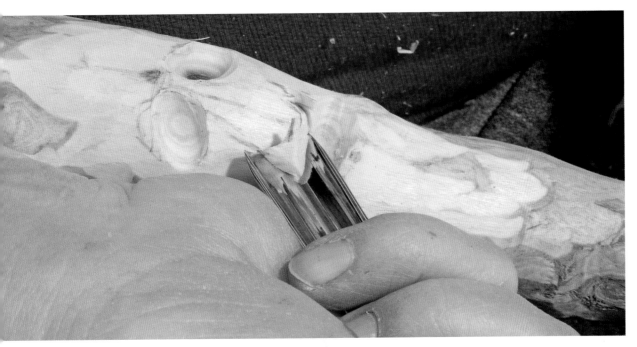

and cut back to it from the lip.

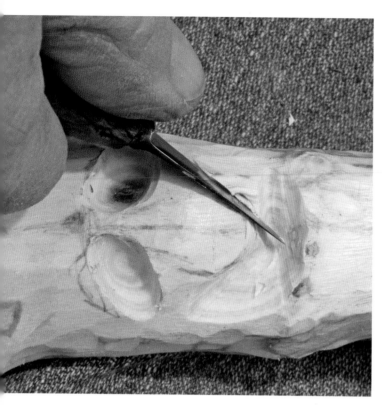 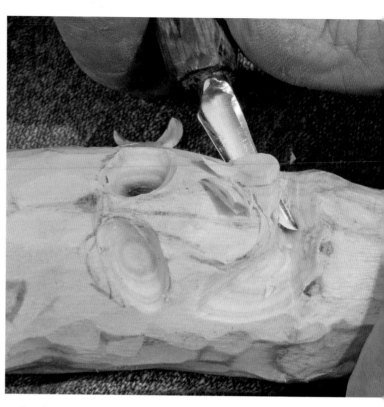

With a knife, cut down beside the nose…

and make scoop-cut back to it from the cheek.

Progress.

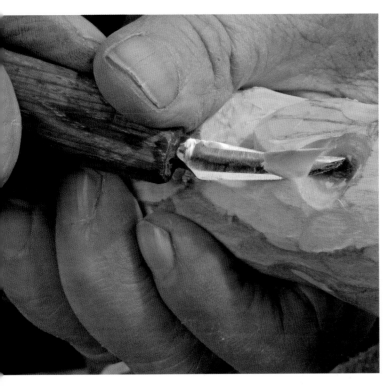

Slice away the area beside the nose to create a perimeter around it.

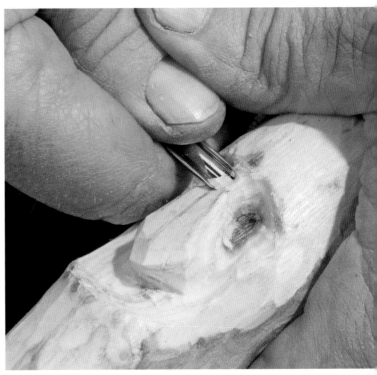

Use the same gouge to cut across the bridge of the nose...

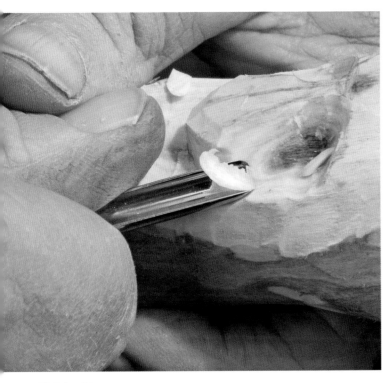

Finish with a gouge.

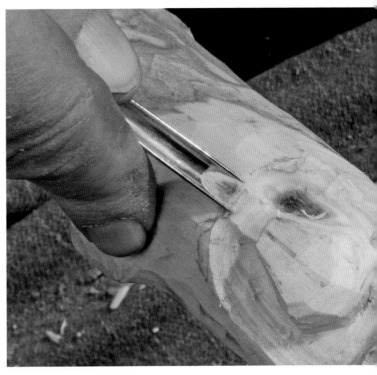

and to separate the brow.

Progress.

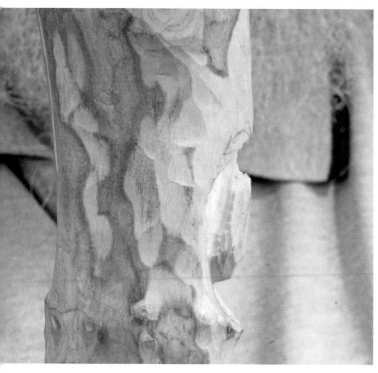

The profile is beginning to emerge.

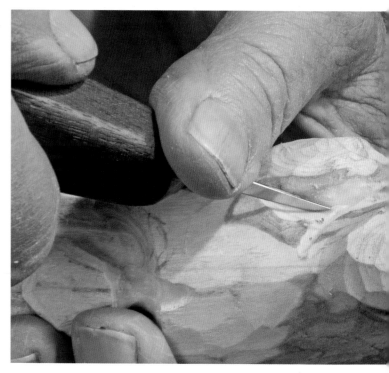

A part in the hairline is created with one stop...

and another.

Cut back into the triangle and pop out the chip.

Progress.

With a v-tool, bring out the hair line.

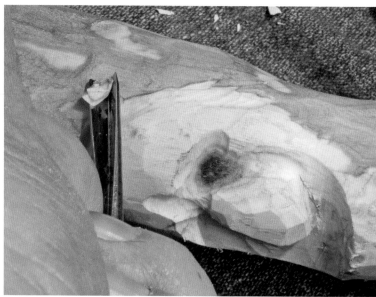

Begin adding hair, here at the top...

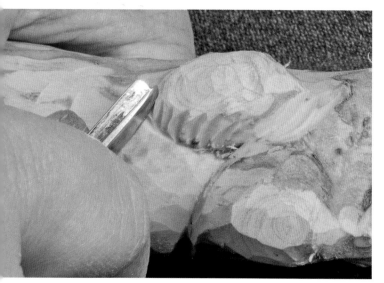

Add some hair lines to one of the bumps on the head. By incorporating these natural shapes you give the carving interest and depth.

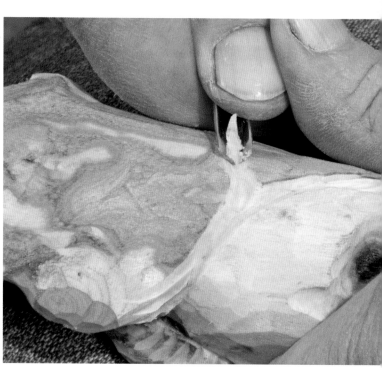

and along the side of the face.

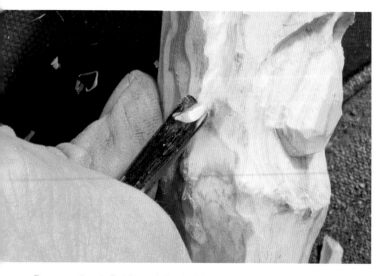

Deepen the definition of the hairline on the right side of the face.

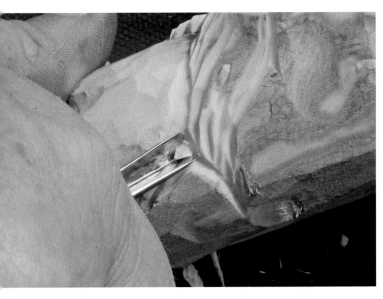

Add a part to the other side, cutting away from the face…

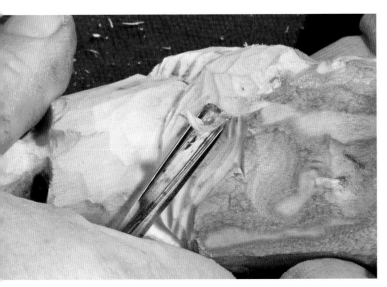

and back.

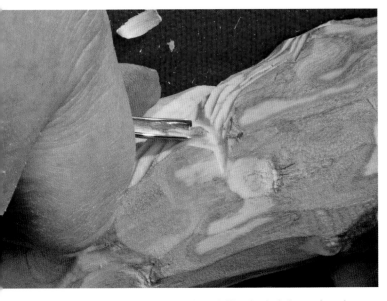

Clean out the triangle, making it look like the hair is turning down.

Make some directional cuts to establish the direction of the hair flow.

Do the same on the side of the face, working up to the part.

Shape the forehead under the hairline.

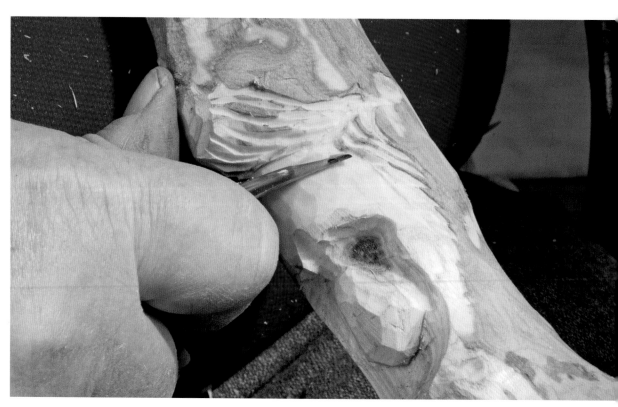

18

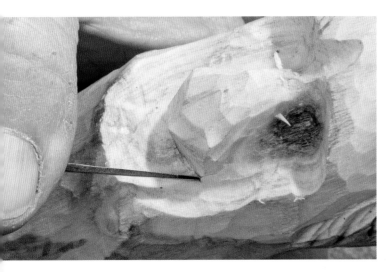

Make a stop beside the nostril…

and another along the cheek line.

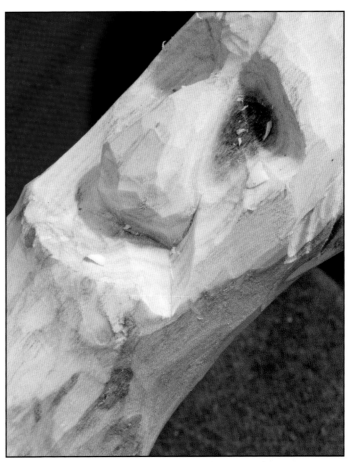

The result.

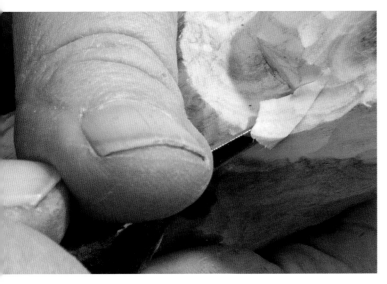

Slice into the triangle from the lip and lift up the chip.

Soften the edge of the moustache.

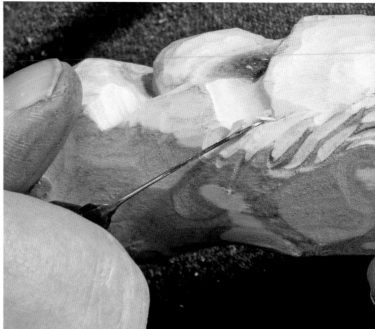

Cut off the chip with a knife.

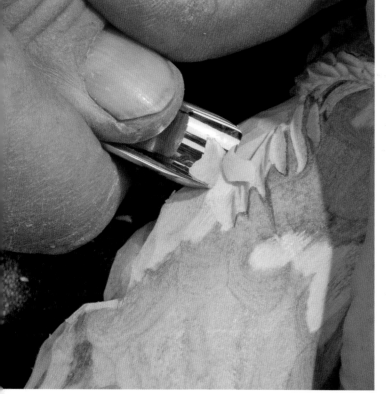

With a large gouge cut from the eye socket into the temple.

The result.

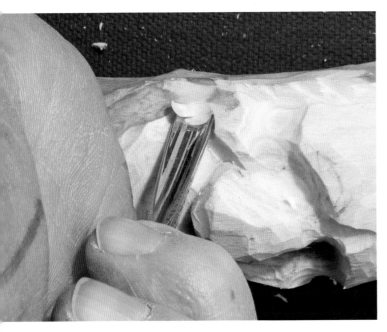

Run the gouge under the cheek to bring out the cheek bone. Start near the upper lip and carry the cut back and up toward the temple.

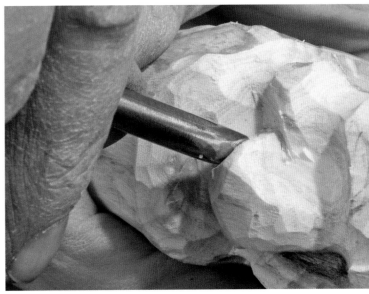

The nostrils are form by pushing a gouge under the nose and straight into the lip.

The result.

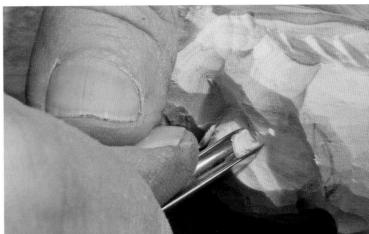

Use the same gouge to go over the outside of the nostril, cutting back to the cheek.

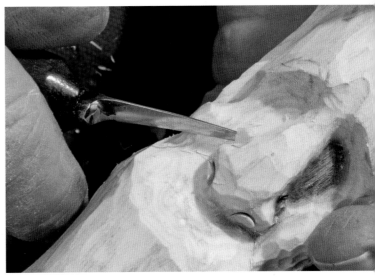

Clip the chip here...

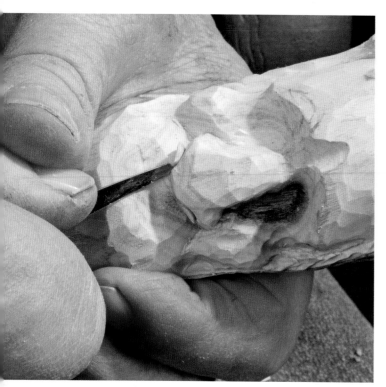

and below the nose.

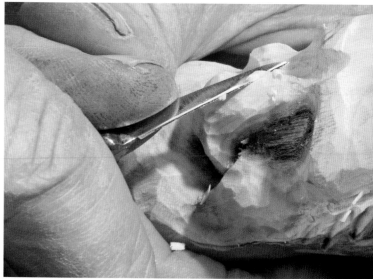

It's a good time to do a little dressing of the nose.

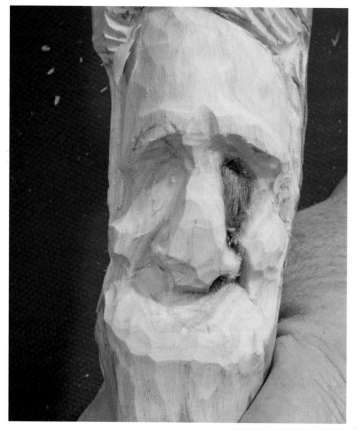

Progress.

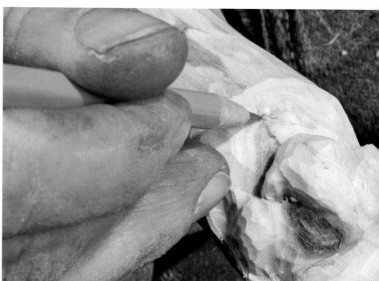

Mark the separation of the moustache...

and its lower edge.

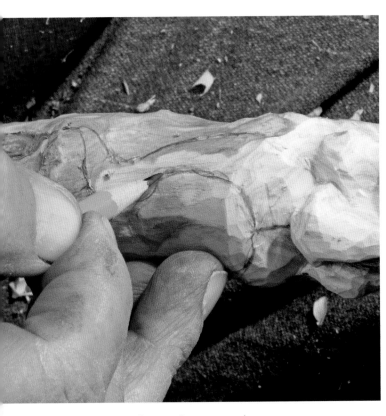

I want a nice long flow to the moustache.

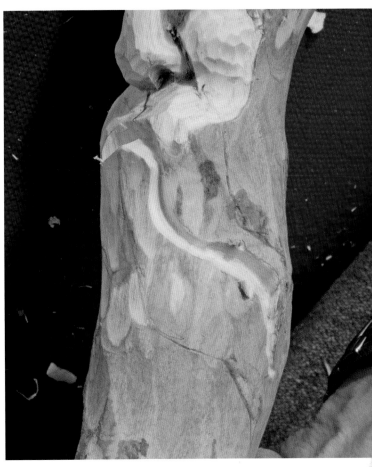

The result.

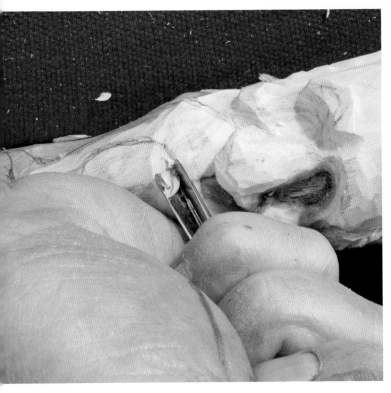

Use a v-tool to undercut the line of the moustache, creating a good deep shadow.

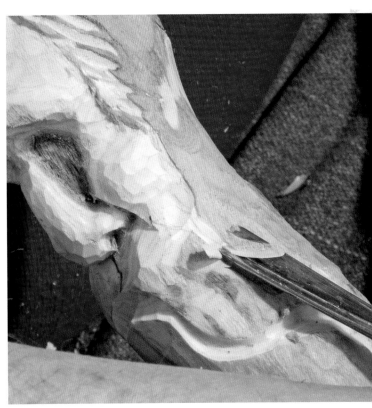

Come back along the upper edge of the moustache so it is outlined.

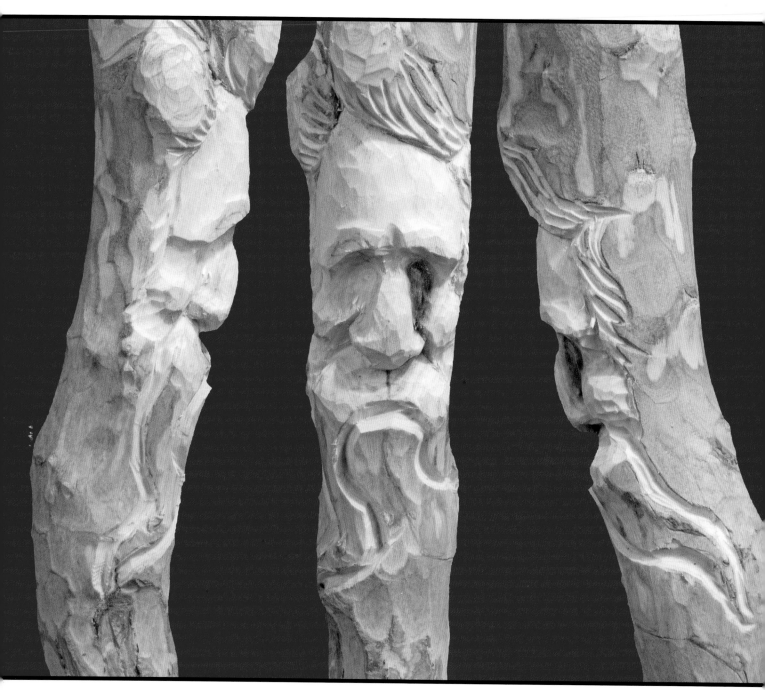

Progress.

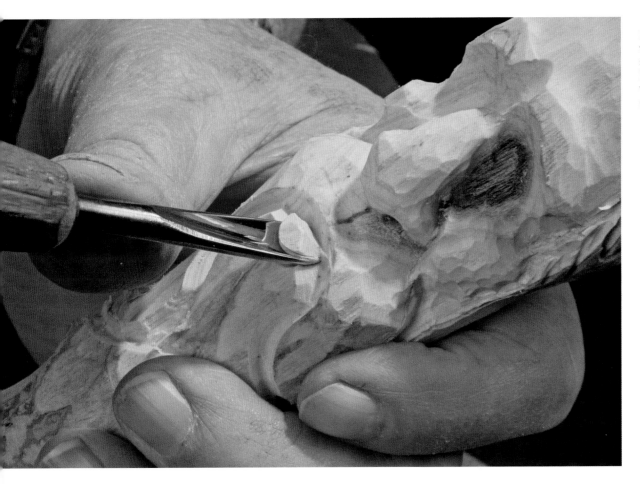

I want the figure
to be blowing
so I push deeply
into the mouth
with a half-round
gouge.

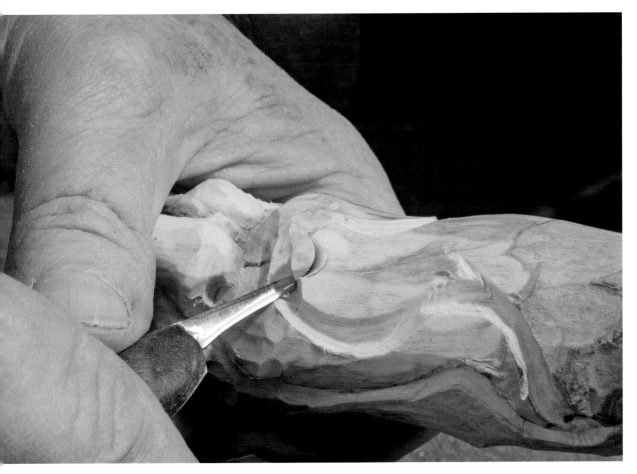

Clip it off...

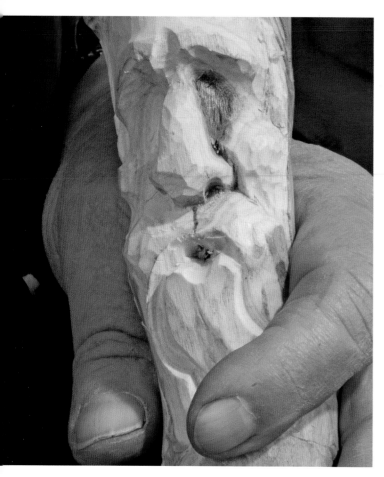

for this result. Deepen the hole. The color that showed up in the left eye, is now put to good purpose as it appears in the mouth.

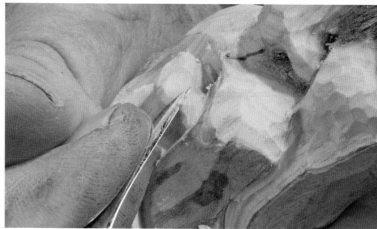

Shape the lip a little bit.

The mouth was a little out of balance so I am taking a little from one side.

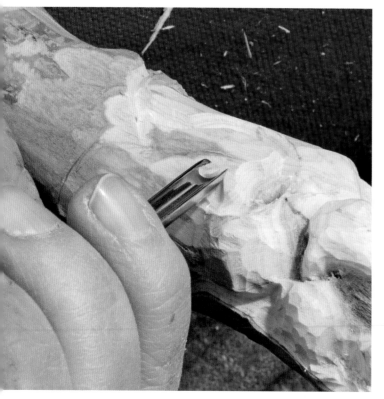

Run the gouge underneath the lower lip to bring it out.

A v-tool will separate the halves of the moustache.

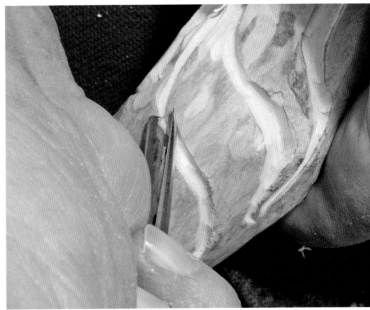

Add some major hairlines to the beard.

Progress.

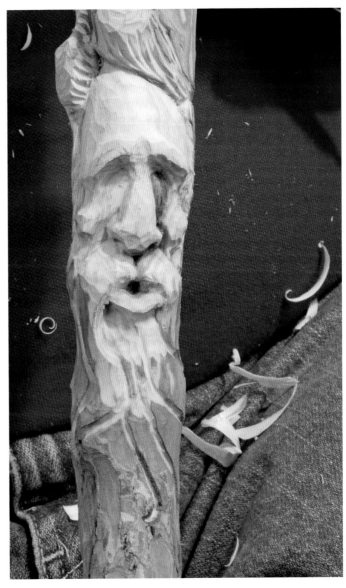

Progress.

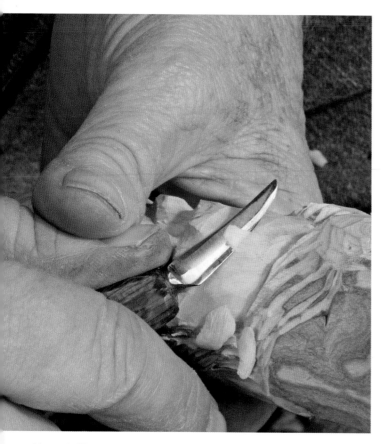

Use a knife to shape the forehead. I want a strong brow line, so scoop out some above. It.

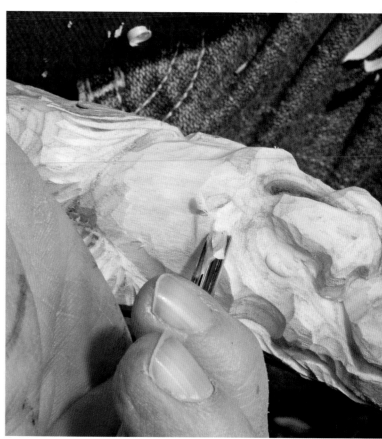

Do the same on the other side.

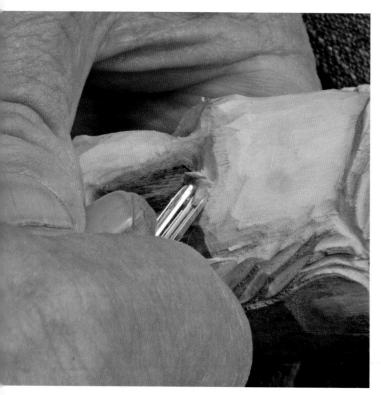

Undercut the eyebrow to give it a blousey look.

The result

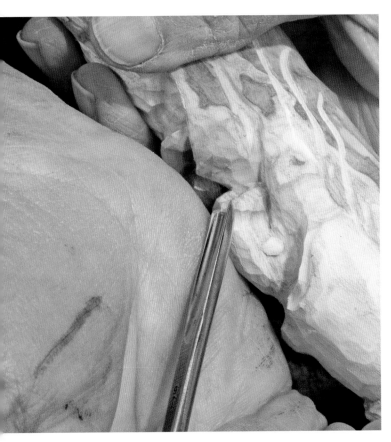

Narrow the nose in front of the nostril.

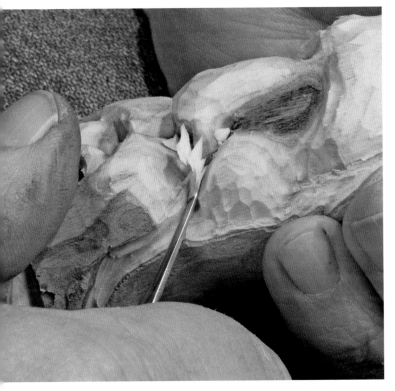

As you go you will see things that need refining, like the space where the cheek meets the nose…

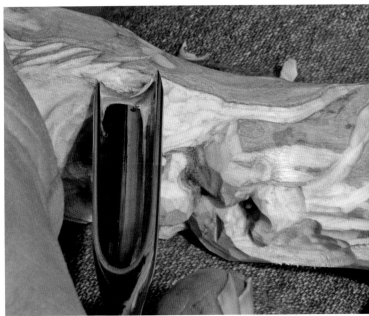

or the fact that the left cheek is higher than the right, which I am fixing here with a gouge.

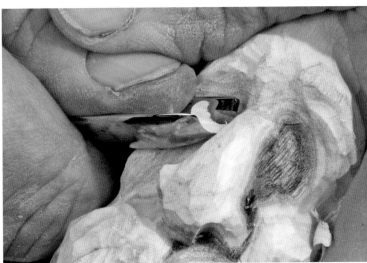

I also want to narrow the bridge of the nose a little bit.

Fill in the details of the hair lines.

I like to use these natural bumps in the carving. Here it makes a great mound of hair.

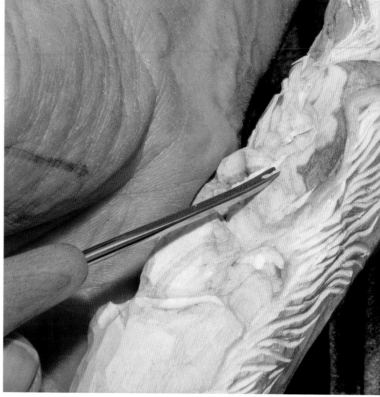

Use a smaller v-tool to add hair to the moustache.

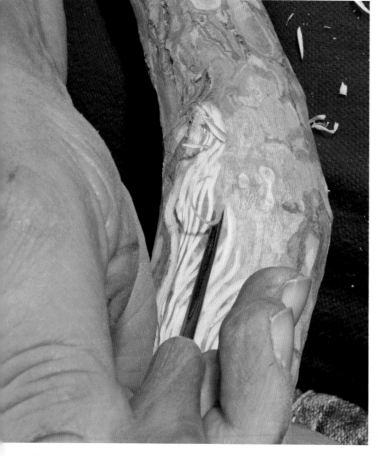

Continue into the beard as well.

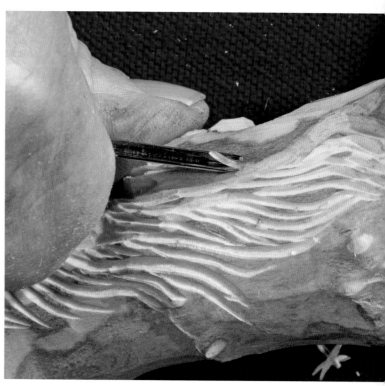

These should be flowing, long lines but the limitations of the tool mean you have to take small strokes and connect them.

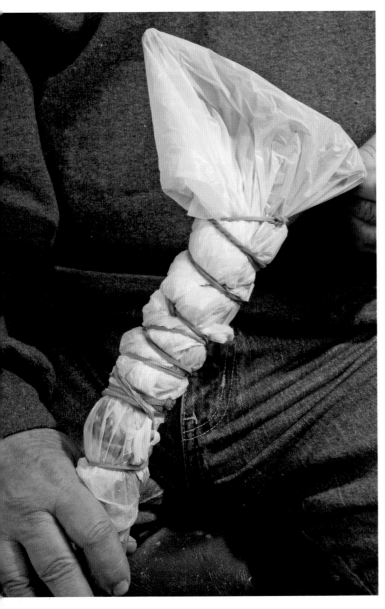

Spritz the wood with a combination of half rubbing alcohol and half water and keep the handle covered at night to keep it moist and soft.

Finish carving the beard with a small v-tool or veiner.

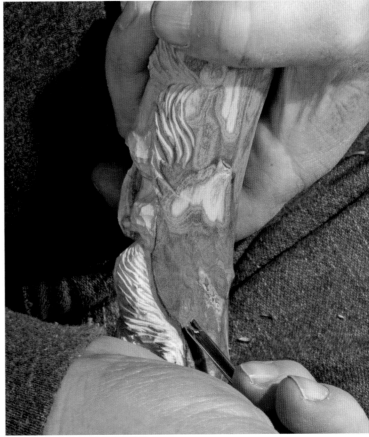

Adding a little hair to this blank area along the side of the head.

Progress.
The hair is carved.

32

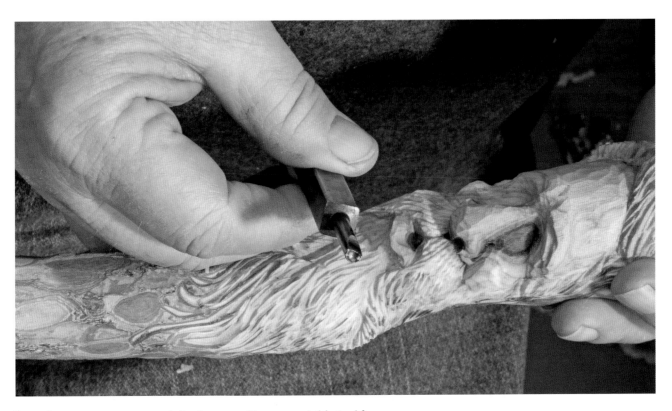

I'm going to use an eye punch for the eyes. You can get this tool from just about any woodcarving supplier.

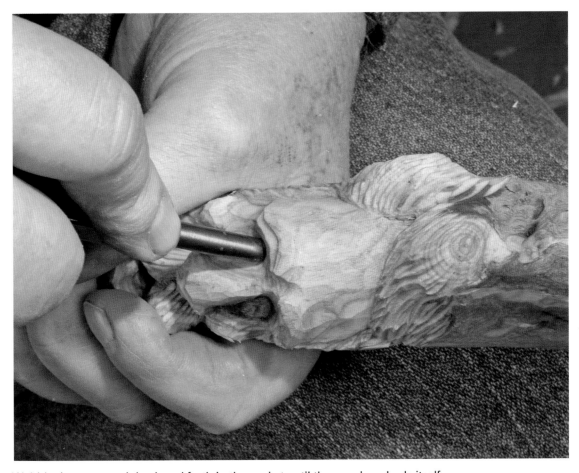

Wobble the eye punch back and forth in the socket until the punch embeds itself.

The punch has created the eyes.

Make three small cuts for the tear duct, one angled away from the upper edge of the eye toward the nose...

the second angled up from the bottom of the eye away from the nose...

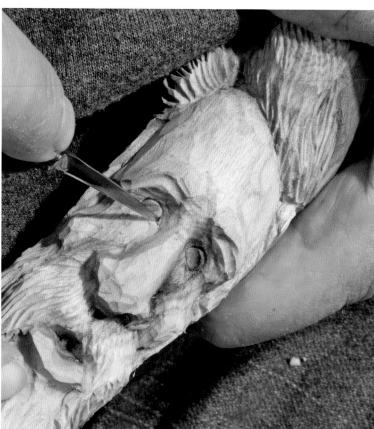

and the third from the edge of the eye itself outward. This should pop out a small triangle of wood. If it doesn't, repeat the cuts and try again. Don't pick at it.

The result.

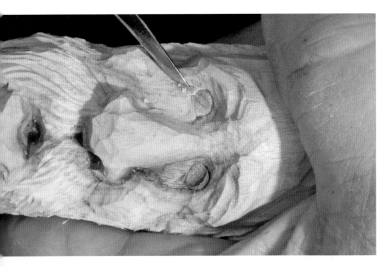

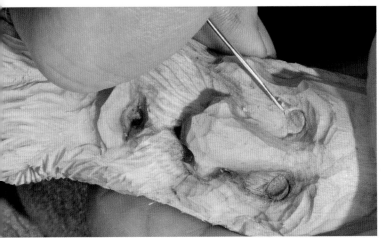

Both sides are finished.

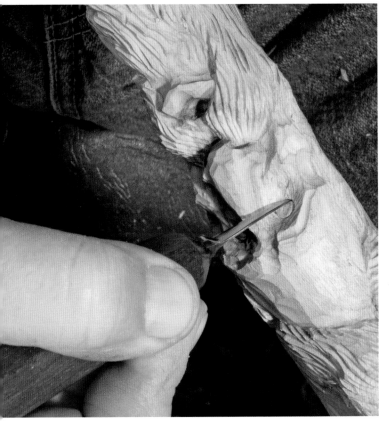

Repeat this process along the outer corner of the eye.

The corners of both eyes carved.

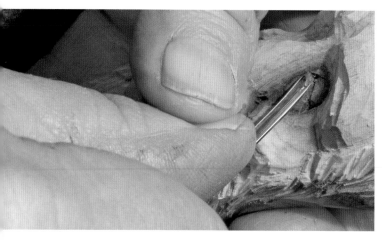

Run a small v-tool under the eye to create the lower eyelid. Work from the center below the eye, first toward the inner corner, and then toward the outer corner.

Repeat this process below the eyelid to create a bag under the eye. Each bag adds twenty years to the figure.

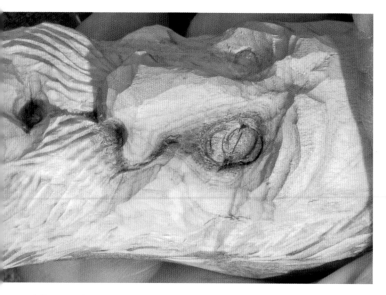

The result.

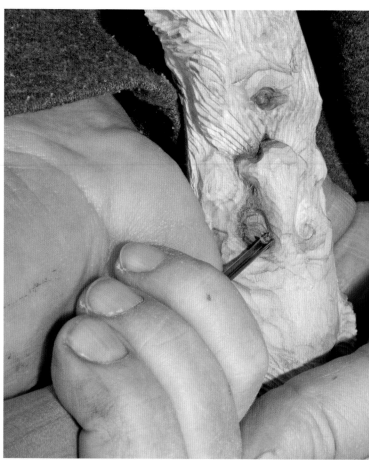

Repeat this process for the upper lid. Make sure to leave a bit of an indent beside the nose to recess the eye a bit.

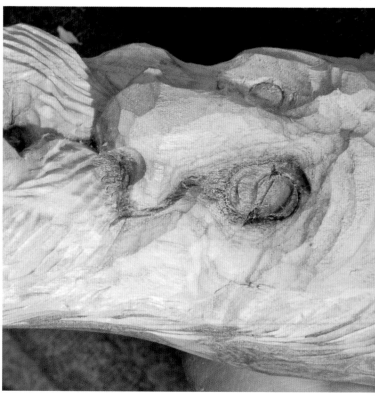

Progress.

Repeat on the other eye for this result.

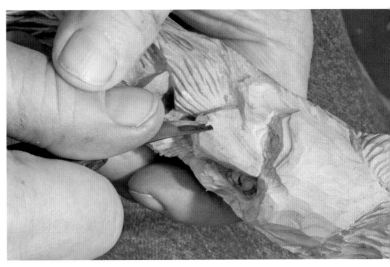

Using a small knife with an upturned blade, smooth out the figure, rounding down the highlights and breaking up any straight lines.

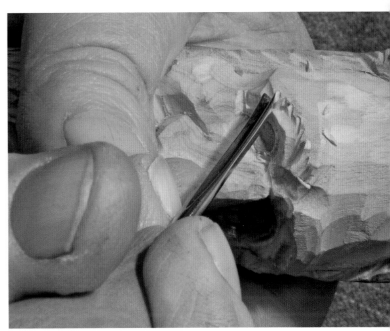

Using the v-tool to add hair lines to the eyebrows.

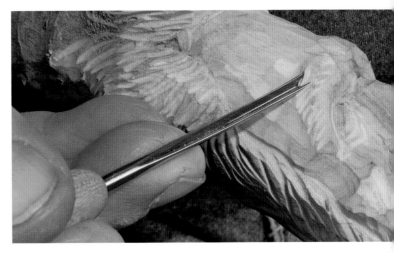

Longish strokes on the eyebrow hair will make them bushy to go along with the bushy hair and beard.

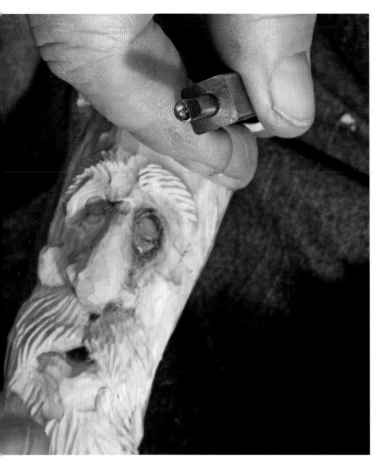

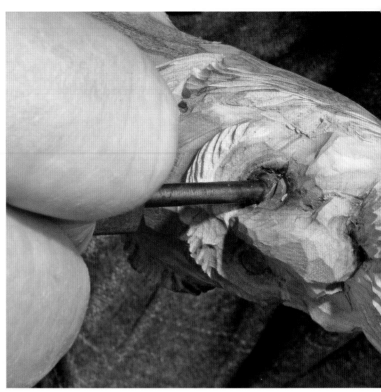

Rock the eyepunch back and forth to crate the line.

The iris is formed with a smaller eyepunch, like that used for the eyeball. Again the top edge is ground off.

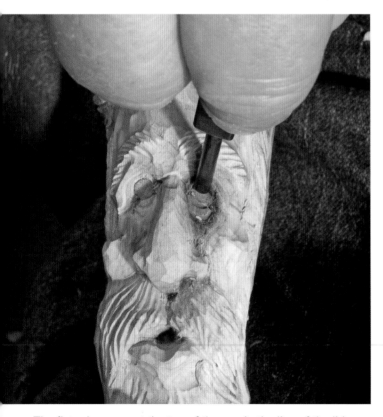

The flat edge goes at the top of the eye in the line of the lid.

The result.

Progress.

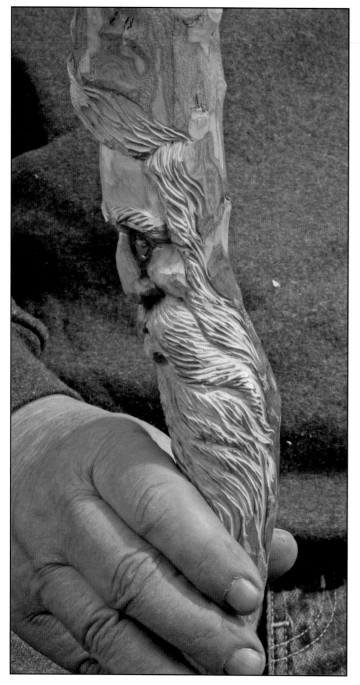

Progress.

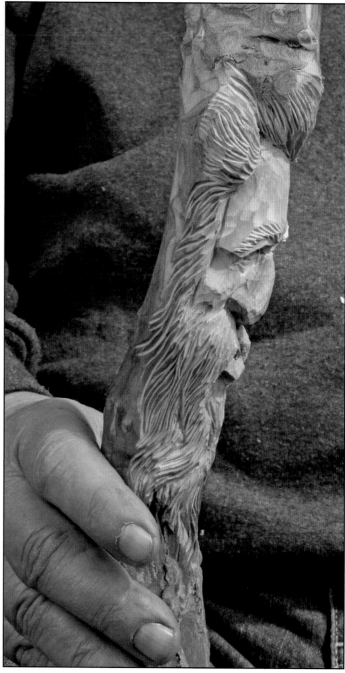

Progress.

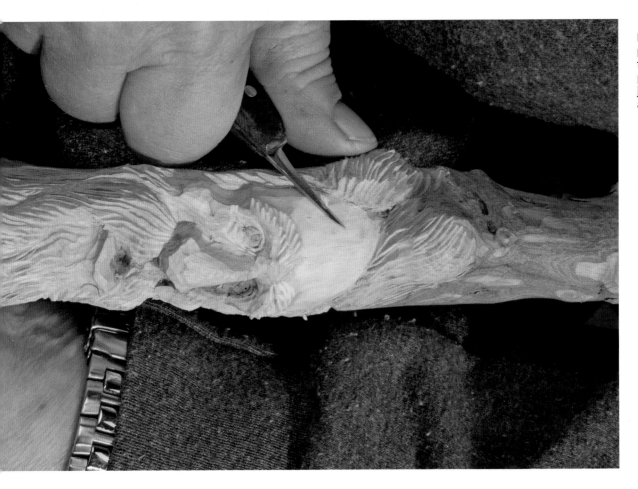

I go over the piece one last time before painting. This is just to clean up any rough spots.

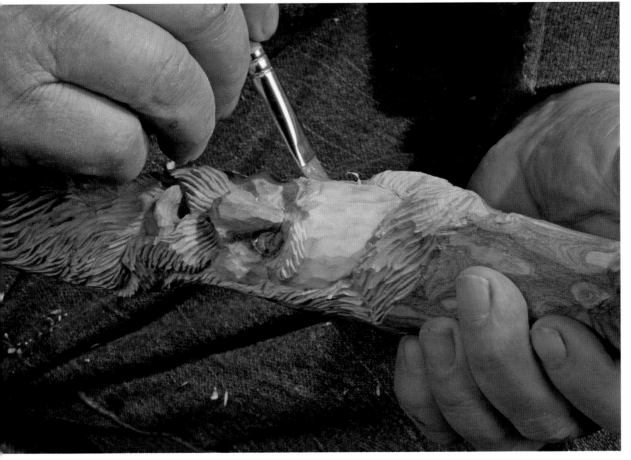

Before painting I apply a coating of turpentine to the carving. This brings the color out in the wood for those parts that aren't receiving paint, that helps the paint penetrate the wood in those areas that are. This is especially important when using paint pencils.

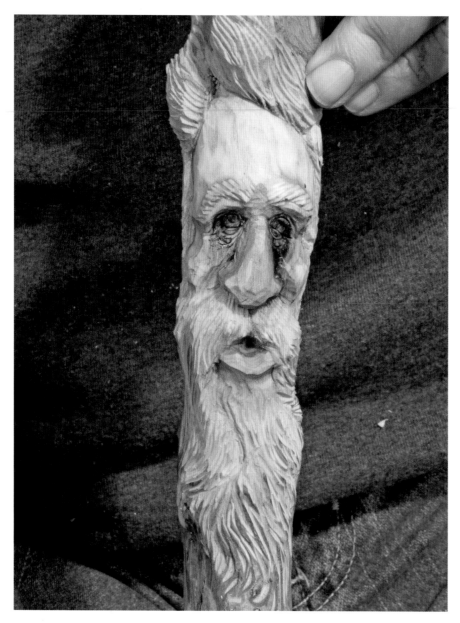

As you have no doubt notice from the beginning, there was a dark vein in the wood that went right through the character's left eye. If not for that, we may have left this carving unpainted. Instead we need to make it look as if it belonged there…part of its character. Using brown and black, I've shaded in the area of the other eye to match the natural staining in the area of the left eye. Now the figure looks natural, with deep-set eyes.

I use paint pencils for much of this work. Made by General, under the Multichrome brand, they give good color and a lot of control if you keep a good, sharp point on them. Before using, soak the pencil in turpentine for a couple of minutes. For this project I'll use Carmine Red, Scarlet Red, White, Dark Blue (Indigo), Light Blue, Van Dyke Brown, and Black. Usually my character's eyes have two colors, dark blue and light blue.

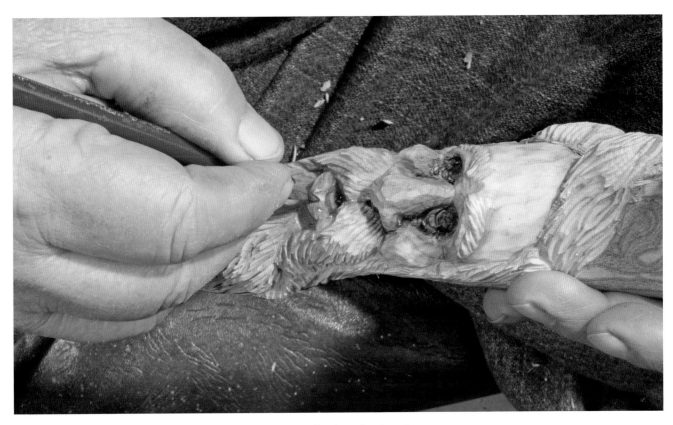

I use Carmine Red on the lip. The pencil gives the muted colors that I prefer, almost like a wash. Add some red to the nose and cheeks, too.

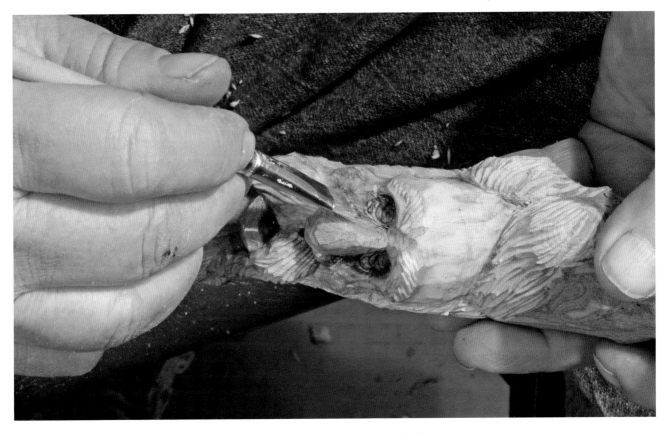

A little turpentine on a brush will blend the colors and wash them out a bit. If it's still too bright, do it again and wash it out some more.

Progress. The Carmine red has washed out more than I like...

The colors are a little richer now..

so I'll add some Scarlet Red to the lips and the highlights of the nose and cheeks. If the color does not apply well, sharpen the point again,

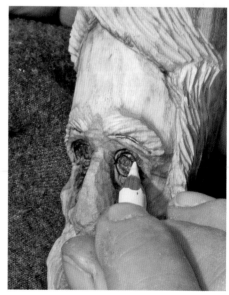

To begin coloring the eyes, use white on the entire surface of the eye first.

44

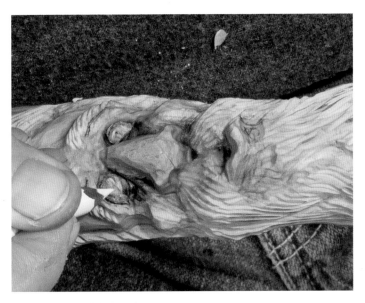

The white is added to the eyes.

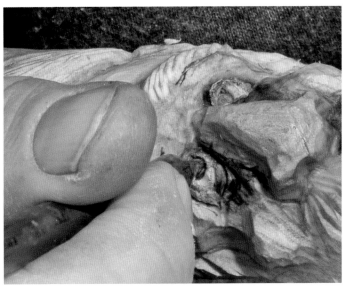

Paint the iris light blue and outline it in dark blue.

Progress.

The eyes are colored.

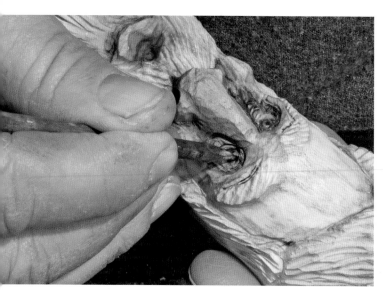

Use a brush handle or a sharp nail to apply black paint to the pupils.

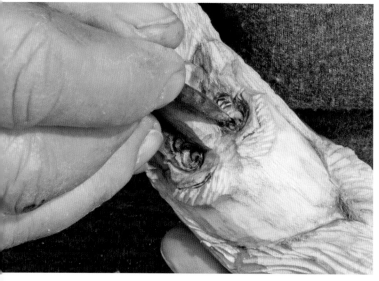

Apply a little white in the same way to lighten things up a bit in the rest of the eye.

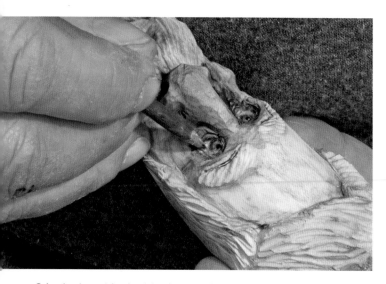

Stipple the white in. It's slow work but accurate.

The eyes are finished.

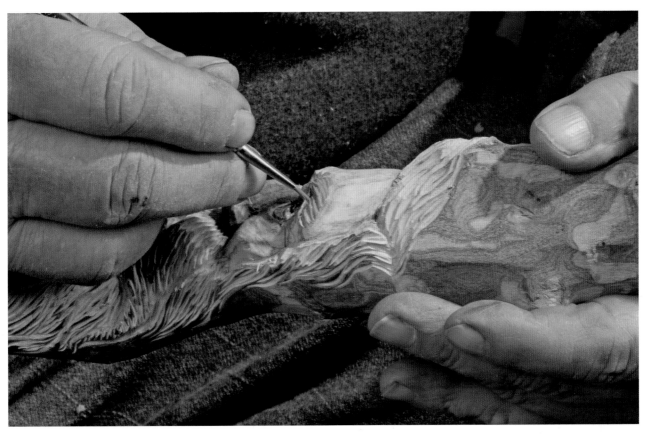

Paint the hair using orange paint. I'm using artist oil paints thinned with turpentine.

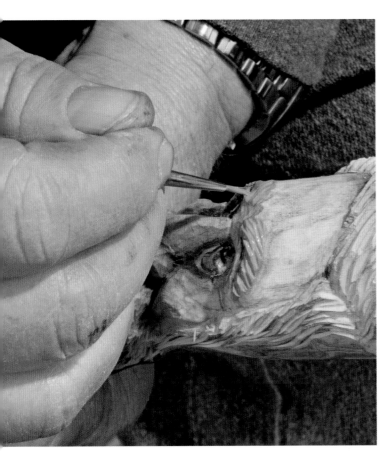

I'll probably use three different colors of paint on the hair before I'm done to get a good red-headed look. Add some yellow to lighten up the hair a bit.

Paint yellow in the hair around the temples.

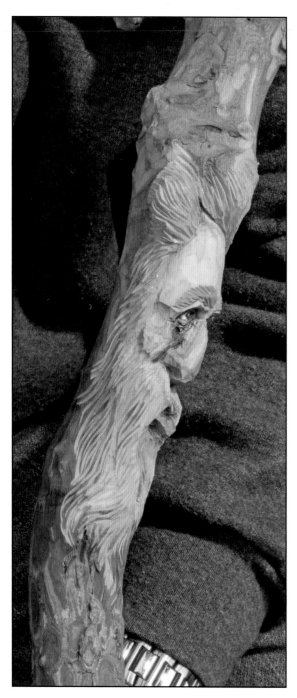

Progress. The hair around the face has been painted with the yellow.

Burnt sienna around the outer edges of the hair and beard helps set it apart from the surrounding wood.

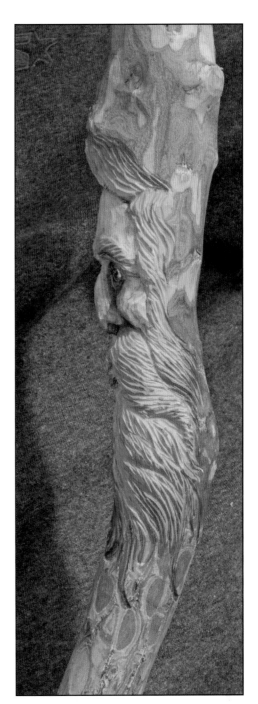

Finally I return to the orange to fill in the remaining area and blend the hair into an interesting whole.

The painting is finished.

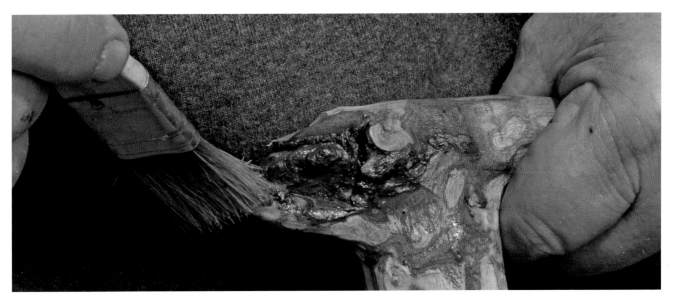

Use the turpentine to clean off the stone embedded in the handle.

Add a finishing coat of Matte finish Krylon 1311. The Krylon matte finish or a Deft spray helps the oil paint to dry more quickly.

Gallery

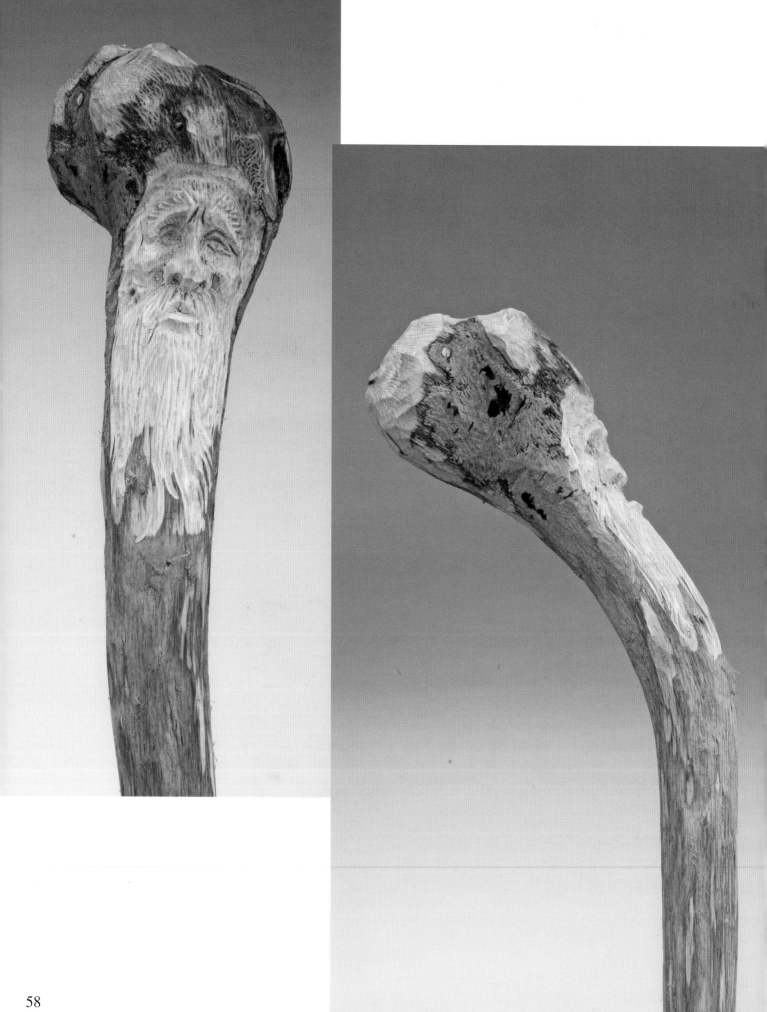

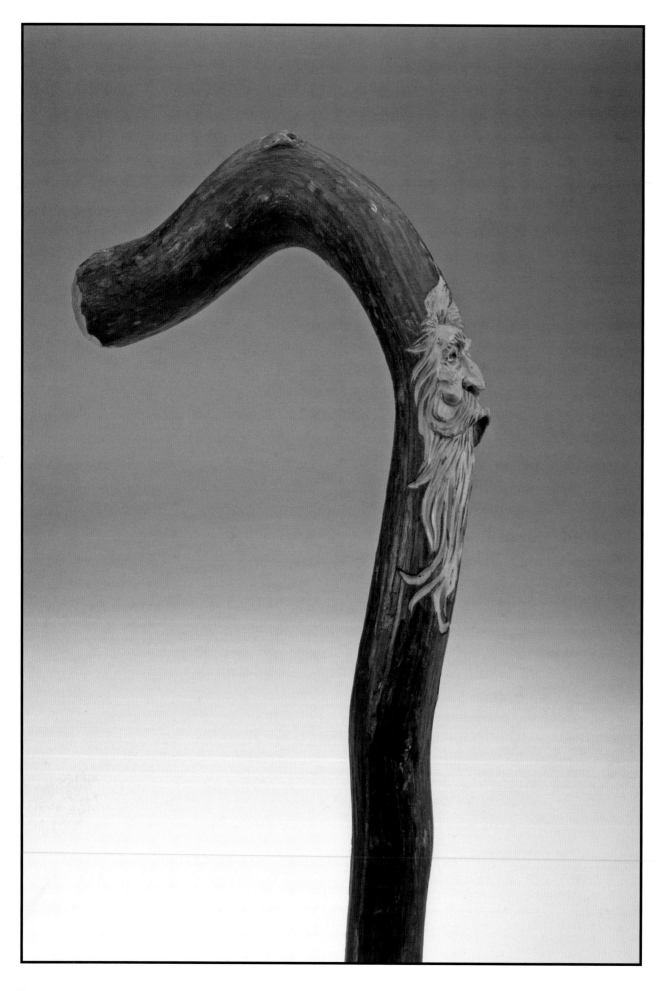